FUN-FACTS THAT FEEL LIKE THEY CAN'T BE TRUE

ARE YOU KIDDING ME?

HARRY BRIGHT AND JAKOB ANSER

MJF BOOKS

NEW YORK

Published by MJF Books
Fine Communications
322 Eighth Avenue
New York, NY 10001

Are You Kidding Me?
LC Control Number: 2009925488
ISBN-13: 978-1-56731-975-0
ISBN-10: 1-56731-975-0

Copyright © 2009 by Harry Bright and Jakob Anser

DESIGNED BY LISA CHOVNICK

Printed in the United States of America.

MJF Books and the MJF colophon are trademarks
of Fine Creative Media, Inc.

MV   10   9   8   7   6   5   4   3   2   1

ARE YOU KIDDING ME?

A Catholic priest came up with the Big Bang theory. Georges Lemaître, a professor of physics and astronomy at the Catholic University of Leuven, Belgium, published his "hypothesis of the primeval atom" in the science journal *Nature* in 1931.

Fred Hoyle, an atheist and astronomer, coined the phrase "Big Bang" during a 1949 radio interview to mock Lemaître's theory of the origin of the universe. Hoyle rejected the implication that the beginning of the universe required a causal agent, i.e. God. He proposed a steady-state theory in which the universe has no beginning or end—a view that has since fallen out of favor.

◆ ◆ ◆ ◆ ◆ ◆ ◆ ◆ ◆ ◆ ◆ ◆ ◆ ◆ ◆ ◆ ◆

You can't burp in space. Gas requires earthly gravity to separate from the liquid in your stomach.

At over four feet long and weighing over a hundred pounds, the South American *capybara* is the largest rodent in the world. In the sixteenth century, the Catholic Church classified it as a fish so that it could be eaten during Lent.

◆ ◆ ◆ ◆ ◆ ◆ ◆ ◆ ◆ ◆ ◆ ◆ ◆ ◆ ◆ ◆

The *zyzzyva* is a tropical American weevil and the last entry in many dictionaries.

Every March, surfers gather along the Amazon River to ride the *pororoca*, or "endless wave." When the tide of the Atlantic Ocean advances into the Amazon River basin, twelve-foot swells race upstream at twenty miles an hour for hundreds of miles. Surfers refer to the *pororoca* as the "Amazonian tsunami." A record-setting ride lasted more than half an hour over a span of seven miles.

◆ ◆ ◆ ◆ ◆ ◆ ◆ ◆ ◆ ◆ ◆ ◆ ◆ ◆ ◆

The Amazon is the largest river in the world. It has no bridges.

The Amazon flows with such force that sailors two hundred miles out to sea can drink fresh water.

The phrase "the bitter end" is a nautical term referring to the "bits" around which cables and ropes are wound. If a rope is played out to the bitters' end, the anchor has likely hit the sea floor and you are out of line.

The phrase "beat the rush" was coined in reference to the revenue clipper ship USS *Rush*, which operated in Alaskan waters in the mid-1800s. Local black-marketers would race to sell undeclared pelts before the ship docked, thereby beating the rush.

The coded information in the chromosomes of a single fertilized human egg contains the equivalent of roughly one thousand printed volumes of books, each as large as a volume of the *Encyclopedia Britannica*.

Bertrand Russell and Alfred North Whitehead's *Principia Mathematica* is a seminal three-volume work on the foundation of mathematics. It contains a 362-page proof concluding that one plus one does indeed equal two.

The onager (*Equus hemionus*), a central Asian species in the horse family, is commonly referred to as the "Asian wild ass" and the "half ass."

The American usage of *half-assed* to mean "ineffectual" or "unplanned" dates back to 1932 and may derive from a playful mispronunciation of *haphazard*.

There are two talking animals in the Old Testament: the serpent in the Garden of Eden (Genesis) and Balaam's talking ass (Numbers).

After ten years of use, seventy percent of the solid weight of your pillow is likely to be dust mite excrement.

Licking your toilet seat may be healthier than typing on your keyboard. Researchers have found that desks on average harbor four hundred times more bacteria than toilet seats.

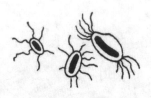

We have more bacteria living inside us than we have cells. The human body contains roughly 100 trillion cells and up to two quadrillion bacteria. An objective observer, such as an extraterrestrial, might reasonably conclude that human beings exist merely to provide homes for bacteria.

The phrase "drop-dead gorgeous" dates back to when a ghostly pallor was thought to be the acme of feminine beauty. To achieve this pale look, women would paint their faces with makeup containing arsenic—a toxic substance that literally caused many beauties to drop dead.

Some bacteria can "breathe" arsenic. Found in hot springs and other environments where oxygen is scarce, these bacteria use arsenic for photosynthesis. Scientists believe that the bacteria's ability to process arsenic evolved billions of years ago, when the planet's oceans were devoid of oxygen.

Elysia chlorotica, a green sea slug native to the eastern seaboard of the United States, is the only known animal that can carry out photosynthesis. The DNA of this solar-powered slug contains one of the same genes found in the algae it eats. This gene allows the sea slug to "steal" chloroplasts—the green cellular objects that enable plant cells to convert sunlight into energy—from the algae and store them in the cells that line its gut. Once this plant-animal hybrid has enough chloroplasts, it can live off sunlight for up to nine months.

◆ ◆ ◆ ◆ ◆ ◆ ◆ ◆ ◆ ◆ ◆ ◆ ◆ ◆ ◆

Naked mole rats are the only known cold-blooded mammals.

Though mammals cannot breathe underwater, they can smell. Some species of moles and shrews blow out bubbles from their noses then quickly re-inhale, sniffing the air inside the bubbles for traces of underwater prey.

Some turtles can breathe through their butts. These butt-breathing turtles have the ability to stay under water for extended periods by sucking water in through their cloacae and passing dissolved oxygen past papillae, similarly to how fish use gills to respire.

Julius Caesar brought the first giraffe to Europe in 46 BC. Romans called it a "cameleopard." Caesar debuted the cameleopard in the arena, where lions tore it to shreds.

The word *arena* is Latin for "dust" or "sand." The floors of arenas—most famously the Coliseum—were covered in sand to soak up spilled blood so that gladiators fighting for their lives wouldn't slip.

The word *scruple* derives from the Latin for "small stone." Having scruples refers to your conscience bothering you as would a pebble in your shoe.

The Ancient Greeks and Romans believed in plurality and disbelieved in nothingness. Believing in the void or even the mathematical concept of zero was heresy and punishable by death.

The words *googol* (the number one with a hundred zeros after it) and *googolplex* (ten raised to the power of one googol) were invented in 1938 by Milton Sirotta, the nine-year-old nephew of mathematician Edward Kasner.

10000000000000000000000000000000000000000000

A googolplex is such a large number that there wouldn't be enough space to write it out even if you traveled to the farthest reaches of the known universe and back putting down zeros every inch of the way.

Two Google searches use enough energy to boil a kettle of water.

It is theoretically possible to travel faster than the speed of light without actually moving. In 1994, the physicist Miguel Alcubierre proposed a warp drive—a concept first popularized by the 1960s television show *Star Trek*—which would expand the fabric of space behind a ship and shrink it in front, thus allowing the craft to essentially surf down the side of a space-time bubble while remaining motionless. Physicists estimate that firing up the warp drive would require an amount of energy using Einstein's equation $E=mc^2$ in which m is equivalent to the mass of Jupiter.

G rey goo" is a hypothetical apocalypse scenario involving nanotechnology in which infinitesimal robots gone haywire consume all matter on Earth while continuously replicating themselves. Nanotechnology pioneer Eric Drexler coined the term for this microscopic Frankenstein phenomenon in his 1986 book *Engines of Creation*.

It takes 29.5 days for the moon to make one full rotation. It also takes 29.5 days for the moon to orbit the Earth. This is why we see the same face of the moon at all times. This hasn't always been true. The moon's spin has gradually slowed down to match its orbit around the Earth.

Technically, the moon does not orbit the Earth. The moon moves around the Earth, but the Earth is also moving. Both celestial bodies orbit a common point called the "barycenter."

The word *yahoo*, meaning a "brute in human form," comes from *Gulliver's Travels*. The Yahoos eschewed reason for the sake of vice and materialism.

In *Gulliver's Travels*, published in 1726, Jonathan Swift described Mars's two moons. Mars does indeed have two moons, Phobos and Deimos, but they weren't discovered until 1877, nearly 150 years after the novel was written.

American frontiersman Daniel Boone often made reference to events in *Gulliver's Travels*, one of his favorite books, and even claimed that he killed a "hairy giant that Swift called a Yahoo." Boone's tale is considered by some to be the source of the Big Foot legend.

Fatal hilarity" is death resulting from uncontrollable laughter. Fatal hilarity starts out as regular laughter, then ends up either in asphyxiation, cardiac arrest, or infarction of the medulla oblongata—tissue death caused by lack of oxygen to the region of the brain stem responsible for involuntary activities like blood pressure and breathing.

The Greek stoic philosopher Chrysippus died of fatal hilarity in the third century BC after getting his donkey drunk on wine and watching it attempt to eat a fig. Self-control is one of the main tenets of stoicism.

Whales descended from hippopotami.

Hippos sweat natural sunscreen. The red-colored secretion is a highly acidic complex compound sometimes referred to as "blood sweat." It is technically neither blood nor sweat.

The elephant is the only mammal
that can't jump.

In 2007, scientists discovered that scent activates memory during sleep. Participants in the experiment were given a rose bouquet to sniff as they studied for an exam—and later as they slept. Those who stopped and smelled the roses did markedly better on the examination than the subjects who did not.

According to a recent study by Dr. Alan Hirsch of the Smell & Taste Treatment and Research Foundation, the combined aroma of lavender and pumpkin pie is the most potent aphrodisiac for men. Baby powder is the top sexually stimulating scent for women.

The human brain cannot distinguish between a sneeze and an orgasm.

For one out of every three people, looking at the sun triggers a sneeze. Neurologists believe that the photic sneeze reflex, or "sun sneeze," is caused by crossed wires in the brain. The trigeminal nerve, which senses the irritation that causes a normal sneeze, is in close proximity to the optic nerve. When the optic nerve gets overloaded, the electrical signal spills over into the trigeminal nerve, thus causing a sneeze.

An itchy nose can indicate lying. When a person lies, tissues in the nose engorge. The nasal swelling isn't as dramatic as Pinocchio's, but it does produce histamine, which in turn causes the nose to itch.

According to the Facial Action Coding System (FACS), which maps all the possible expressions of the forty-three facial muscles, there are at least fifty kinds of smiles. Fox Television's *Lie to Me* is based on the professional life of Dr. Paul Ekman, co-developer of FACS.

Smiling predicts success in marriage. After poring over family photos and rating the smiles of their test subjects, psychologists have determined that ninety percent of the biggest smilers stay married, while roughly thirty percent of the frowners get divorced.

Women smile more than men.

In 2007, a nine-year-old boy from northern England had an abscess removed from his brain. After the surgery, he awoke speaking the Queen's English, having completely lost his Yorkshire accent.

In the same year, a Czech speedway rider knocked out in a crash woke up speaking perfect English, a language he had never learned.

Featured in the "Euphoria" episode of the TV series, *House, M.D.*, Anton-Babinski syndrome is a rare symptom of damage to the occipital lobe, the visual processing center of the brain. Sufferers are blind but adamantly claim to be able to see, even in the face of clear evidence to the contrary, such as walking into walls or describing people who aren't present.

Anton-Babinski syndrome is the converse of blindsight, an oxymoron used to describe the phenomenon of blindness in the mind but not the eyes. More than thirty areas in the human brain are involved in handling aspects of vision, such as the perception of motion, color, and depth. Damage to any one area may affect conscious awareness of what we can or cannot "see."

In 2008, an Irishman blinded by an explosion had his sight restored after doctors inserted his son's tooth into his eye. Osteo-odonto-keratoprosthesis (OOKP), commonly referred to as the "tooth eye surgery," creates an artificial cornea from the canine tooth and part of the surrounding bone.

A German shepherd's sense of smell is over thirty thousand times more acute than a human's. When a German shepherd sticks its head out of the window of a moving car, it is exposed to so many smells it experiences a high equivalent to a human on cocaine.

Guitar legend Eric Clapton and serial killer Ted Bundy each grew up believing his mother was his older sister.

◆ ◆ ◆ ◆ ◆ ◆ ◆ ◆ ◆ ◆ ◆ ◆ ◆ ◆ ◆

Rocking" and "rolling," as well as the term "nitty-gritty," were all African-American euphemisms for sex in the early twentieth century. When radio DJ Alan Freed named the music he played on his show "rock and roll," it was partly to see how much he could get away with vis-à-vis the FCC.

A recent study published in *Science* found that there is a direct link between physical and emotional warmth. Holding something warm makes you feel more generous toward others, while holding something cold makes you more selfish.

The only thing left in the box after Pandora opened it was hope.

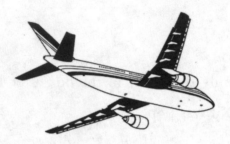

An airplane's flight data recorder, commonly known as the black box, is actually orange.

Viagra reduces jet lag. Based on experiments with hamsters, scientists believe that small doses of Viagra—small enough to avoid any embarrassing "side effects"—may neutralize jet lag in humans.

Alice Denham is the only woman whose fiction and breasts have appeared in the same issue of *Playboy*.

Ninety-five percent of all shoplifters are female.

According to a 2008 study, males who do their share of domestic chores have more sex than their shirking counterparts.

On Valentine's Day at the Toronto Zoo, visitors are invited to watch the animals in captivity mate.

St. Patrick, patron saint of Ireland, was British.

The French horn comes from Germany.

German chocolate cake is not German. The recipe originates from 1950s Texas, and utilizes Baker's German's Sweet Chocolate, named after the Englishman Samuel German.

The word *boycott* comes from Captain Charles Boycott, who managed the affairs of an absentee English landlord in Ireland in the late 1800s. When Boycott refused to lower the rents of his tenant farmers, the Irish Land League made an example of him by treating him like a social leper.

The original Monopoly game, called the Landlord's Game, was intended as a critique of capitalism.

Mortgage literally means "death grip" or "death pledge." The deal dies when all payments are made or when the mortgage holder can no longer make them.

At the peak of the Japanese real estate bubble in 1989, the emperor's Imperial Palace, a compound about the size of New York City's Central Park, was worth more than all the real estate in the state of California.

Queen Elizabeth II is the largest landowner in the world. As the head of state of the United Kingdom and thirty-one other states and territories, she is the legal owner of nearly 6,600 million acres of land, roughly one sixth of the world's landmass. Her holdings, which include entire counties like Canada and Australia, are owned in trust and cannot be sold for her personal benefit.

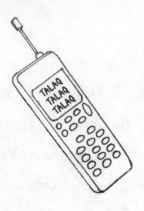

Under Islamic Sharia law, a man can divorce his wife simply by saying the word *talaq* ("I divorce you") three times. A recent court case in Malaysia extended this right to divorce via text message, as long as the text is "clear and unambiguous."

Muslim women are not allowed to congregate with men who are not family members, so holding a job is difficult. To rectify this societal problem, a Muslim cleric issued a breast-suckling *fatwa* in 2007, which states that if a woman offers her breasts to a strange man five times, he is considered family.

Unlike the Catholic Church, for example, Islam has no central doctrinal authority. As a result, religious rulings, or *fatwas*, are nonbinding, leaving the faithful free to look around for better interpretations.

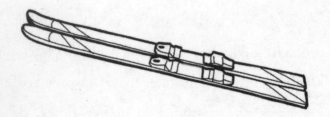

Ski Dubai is one of the largest indoor ski resorts in the world. An insulation system keeps the temperature just below freezing, while the desert beyond its walls burns at 120°F.

The builders of the Els Club golf course at Dubai Sports City in Dubai imported sand from Saudi Arabia for the sand traps. Although Dubai lies within the Arabian Desert, its sand is too symmetrical. Perfect sand traps require angular grains of sand so that golf balls roll to the bottom rather than sticking in the wall of the bunker.

◆ ◆ ◆ ◆ ◆ ◆ ◆ ◆ ◆ ◆ ◆ ◆ ◆ ◆ ◆ ◆

Teddy Roosevelt saved football and helped found the NCAA. When eighteen football players died during the 1905 season, the public clamored to ban the sport. An ardent fan, President Roosevelt used the bully pulpit to institute rules outlawing dirty play and excessive brutality. The new rules also introduced the forward pass and set the first down at ten yards instead of five. Roosevelt's involvement led to the formation of a stronger governing body, the Intercollegiate Athletic Association, which later became the NCAA.

When enlisting in 1898, ten of the Rough Riders—the soldiers who fought with Teddy Roosevelt in Cuba—wrote "Football Player" in the space provided for occupation.

In a protest at the tumultuous 1968 Democratic National Convention, legendary Alabama football coach Paul "Bear" Bryant received 1.5 electoral votes for nomination for president— even though he wasn't on the ballot.

Upon Spiro Agnew's resignation in 1973, Gerald Ford, then minority leader of the House of Representatives, became the first vice president to take office under the Twenty-fifth Amendment. Nine months later, Nixon resigned and Ford became president before ever stepping foot into the vice president's official residence at Number One Observatory Circle.

In 1972, California governor Ronald Reagan pardoned Merle Haggard for his past crimes. While doing a fifteen-year stretch at San Quentin State Prison for armed robbery, Haggard attended three of Johnny Cash's concerts there.

Hollywood was founded when Midwestern pioneers Horace and Daeida Wilcox subdivided their ranch in order to create a community based on sober religious principles.

◆ ◆ ◆ ◆ ◆ ◆ ◆ ◆ ◆ ◆ ◆ ◆ ◆ ◆ ◆

In the early 1990s, comedian Leo Gallagher's younger brother Ron asked for permission to perform using Gallagher's old material, including his trademark Sledge-O-Matic routine. Gallagher granted his blessing on the condition that his brother made it clear to audiences that *Ron* Gallagher was putting on the show. But Ron began blurring the line between the two acts, often promoting his own as "Gallagher Too." In 2000, Gallagher sued his brother for trademark violations and false advertising. The court decided in favor of Leo Gallagher, but Gallagher's family sided with Ron. As a consequence, Gallagher (the *real* Gallagher) is now estranged from his parents and siblings.

◆ ◆ ◆ ◆ ◆ ◆ ◆ ◆ ◆ ◆ ◆ ◆ ◆ ◆ ◆ ◆

Dave Freeman, co-author of the travel guide *100 Things to Do Before You Die*, only managed to tick off fifty of the items on his best-selling bucket list before he died in an accident at age forty-seven.

The phrase "tongue in cheek" originates with minstrels who sang and danced for eighteenth-century Spanish courts. A duke displeased with the minstrels' silly performances would routinely stick his tongue to the side of his cheek as a public form of silent chastisement.

The first Japanese geisha were men.

Both Russia and England have instituted beard taxes. During the reign of Queen Elizabeth I (1558–1603), whiskers were in vogue, so the treasury instituted a beard tax to raise revenues for Britain's many war efforts. In 1698, Peter the Great attempted to civilize the Russian Empire by forcing his subjects to cut off their beards or pay a fine.

In a paper titled "Mirror, Mirror on the Wall: The Effect of Time Spent Grooming on Wages," economists Jayoti Das and Stephen DeLoach conclude that men can increase their weekly wages by six percent for every extra ten minutes a day they spend grooming.

According to Leviticus, shaving one's beard is a sin. Getting a tattoo or wearing a cotton-poly T-shirt (or any garment of mixed fiber) will also incur God's wrath.

In 1631, Robert Barket and Martin Lucas, the royal printers in London, published a King James Bible with a couple of egregious errors. *The Wicked Bible*, as it has become known, left the word *not* out of the seventh commandment so that it read, "Thou *shalt* commit adultery." A second error read, "the lord hath shewed us his glory and his great arse," instead of "the lord hath shewed us his glory and his greatness" (Deuteronomy 5:24).

Barket and Lucas were fined £300, the equivalent of about $60,000 in today's dollars, and lost their printing license. All but eleven of the one thousand printed copies of *The Wicked Bible* were destroyed. In 2008, one of the surviving copies went on the market for $89,500.

Philip M. Parker, according to himself, is the world's most prolific author, with over two hundred thousand "books" to his name. Using computer algorithms, he generates text much in the way Henry Ford produced cars—a comparison he endorses.

In 2007, "The Last Messages," the world's first text-message novel was published. The 332-page book tells the story of a Finnish information-technology executive who resigns from his job and travels throughout Europe and India, keeping in touch with his friends and relatives along the way. The approximately one thousand texts are rife with grammatical errors and abbreviations commonly used in regular SMS missives.

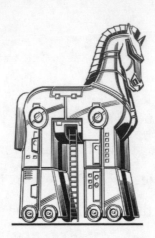

The Play of Chess, published in 1474, was the second book ever published in English. The first, *The Recuyell of the Histories of Troy*, was a collection of stories loosely based on the tales of the Trojan War.

The first book Gutenberg published was not the Bible. It was the *Ars Grammatica*, a dour twenty-eight-page primer on Latin grammar, published sometime around 1450. Gutenberg decided to publish the Bible because he was looking for a best seller.

A lipogram is a piece of writing in which a particular letter or group of letters is intentionally avoided, usually a common vowel. Adam Adams's *Unhooking a DD-Cup Bra without Fumbling* (2008) is a 248-page whodunit that omits *e*, the most common letter in English.

Bollywood film musical vocalist Asha Bhosle is the most recorded singer in history, with over fifty thousand songs to her credit. Her only competition is her older sister Lata Mangeshkar, who held the record until 1991.

The Taj Mahal in Agra, India, was built as a tribute to Shah Jahan's third wife, Mumtaz Mahal, who died in childbirth. After it was completed, the Shah (1592–1666) was deposed and imprisoned by his son, Aurangzeb, who forced his father to live out the rest of his life in a cell—one that offered a view of his majestic creation.

The 2004 Indian Ocean earthquake that caused the deadliest tsunami on record released 550 million times more energy than the Hiroshima bomb, or enough energy to power the United States for 370 years. The explosion was so powerful that it altered the Earth's rotation, shortening the length of the day by 2.68 microseconds.

The King and I is banned in Thailand because it contains historical and cultural distortions. Anna Leonowens was employed as a school teacher, not a governess of the royal children, and rarely had an audience with King Rama IV, much less danced with him.

America calls itself the land of the free—the phrase is in the national anthem—but the word *Thailand* literally means "land of the free."

Croatia means "tie-land." *Hravat,* the Serbo-Croatian word for "Croat," is the origin of cravat, the forerunner to our modern tie. Croatian mercenaries brought their military style of wearing a cravat around the neck to Paris in the 1630s when King Louis XIII enlisted them to support his power struggle against his own mother, Marie de Medici.

In the mid-1700s, the flowing cravat was reintroduced by British "macaroni," stylish and well-educated young men who were the metrosexuals of their time. The word was co-opted from the Italian *maccherone*, meaning "a boorish fool," and anything that was in fashion was said to be "macaroni."

Yankee Doodle stuck "a feather in his cap and called it macaroni." British military officers came up with this ditty to mock the disheveled and disorganized "Yankees" with whom they served in the French and Indian War (1754–1763). *Doodle* was seventeenth-century slang for a fool or simpleton, the joke being that the Yankees were so dumb that they thought sticking a feather in their hat was stylish.

The nursery rhyme "Ring around the Rosy"—"Ring around the rosy, a pocketful of posies, ashes, ashes, we all fall down!"—is about bubonic plague. The symptoms of the plague included a rosy red rash in the shape of a ring on the skin. Posies were carried to combat transmission of the disease. The ashes refer to the cremation of dead bodies.

The word "bank" comes from the Italian *banca*, meaning "bench." In fifteenth-century Venice, Jewish moneylenders were not allowed to own property, so they conducted their business on benches in the piazza.

The word "credit" comes from the Latin *credo*, meaning "I believe," as in "I believe you will pay me back."

Berkshire Hathaway CEO Warren Buffett cheekily christened his corporate jet *The Indefensible*. Once he got used to flying in it, however, he renamed it *The Indispensable*.

Tiger Woods named his 155-foot yacht *Privacy*.

The Anglo-Zanzibar War of August 27, 1896, is the shortest war in recorded history. In just thirty-eight minutes, the Sultan's nephew effected a *coup d'etat*, the British navy gave an ultimatum then attacked, and the nephew fled. As a final humiliation, the British demanded payment for the shells they fired.

On March 1, 2007, Switzerland invaded Liechtenstein when 170 infantry soldiers from the famously neutral country accidentally marched over its unmarked border with the tiny principality. The Swiss troops quickly turned back when they realized their mistake. An interior ministry spokesman from Liechtenstein said no one had even noticed.

Swiss company Romain Jerome SA sells exclusive watches that are partially built from authentic parts of the *Titanic*, which sank in 1912. Prices range from $7,800 to $173,100.

In 1932, the poet Hart Crane drowned when he jumped off an ocean liner. Crane's father Clarence originally held the patent for Life Saver candy.

Catalans have a scatological take on the traditional Christmas Yule log. Children with sticks whack the *caga tio* ("crap log")—a log painted with a broad smiling face and covered with a blanket—all the while singing "Caga, tio, caga!" ("Crap, log, crap!"). If the children have been good, parents reach under the blanket to dole out "crap" in the form of candy, nuts, and nougat.

In Barcelona, Catalonia's capital city, one will also find nativity scenes that lodge among the shepherd, magi, Mary, and Baby Jesus figurines the *caganer* ("crapper"), a gnome-like creature in a red hat squatting over a cone of excrement. In recent years, the *caganer* tradition has been extended to include other characters. Salvador Dalí, Osama bin Laden, and Barack Obama have all assumed the "crapper" position.

President Barack Obama is a distant cousin of both Dick Cheney and George Bush.

In 2009, the descendants of Geronimo, the legendary Apache warrior, filed suit against Skull and Bones, the Yale secret society. They claimed that Prescott S. Bush—grandfather of President George W. Bush—broke into Geronimo's grave in 1918 and made off with Geronimo's skull, two bones, and some other artifacts, all of which ended up on display in "The Tomb," the Skull and Bones clubhouse.

In 2007, Rev. Al Sharpton, Jr., the frequent Democratic campaigner and Civil Rights activist, discovered that relatives of Strom Thurmond, the pro-segregationist, arch-conservative U.S. senator from South Carolina, had owned some of his ancestors.

Out of an "abundance of caution," President Obama retook the presidential oath after Chief Justice John Roberts botched it during the inauguration ceremonies. Language evolutionist Steven Pinker speculated that Roberts, a known grammar gremlin, is constitutionally indisposed to splitting the infinitive "to execute" with the adverb "faithfully." Round two found both Roberts and Obama pronouncing "to faithfully execute," as it is written in the Constitution.

In 2009, President Obama nominated New Hampshire Senator Judd Gregg as commerce secretary. Earlier in his career, Gregg voted to abolish the United States Department of Commerce. Gregg ultimately withdrew his name from nomination citing "irreconcilable differences."

◆ ◆ ◆ ◆ ◆ ◆ ◆ ◆ ◆ ◆ ◆ ◆ ◆ ◆ ◆ ◆

If you spent seven million dollars a week every week since the birth of Christ, you'd have spent less than the American Recovery and Reinvestment Act will cost American taxpayers between 2009 and 2019.

If you invested one penny at the time of Christ's birth and earned five percent interest per year, by 1466 you would have had enough money to buy a ball of gold equal to the weight of the Earth.

The Earth weighs 5.972 sextillion (5,972,000,000,000,000,000,000) metric tons.

Humans have thus far mined a total of 158,000 metric tons of gold. This would fit into a sphere with a diameter of roughly eighty feet.

The vegetables your grandmother told you to eat are no longer available in grocery stores. A recent study published in the *Journal of HortScience* revealed that the average vegetable found in American supermarkets is anywhere from five to forty percent lower in minerals and nutrients than those harvested just fifty years ago.

In 2008, the Food and Drug Administration declared that food from cloned animals and their progeny is safe, in effect making it legal to sell meat and milk derived from copies of prize dairy cows and hogs.

There is a higher percentage of water in cucumbers than in whole milk.

Some strawberry yogurt and cranberry juices get their deep red coloring from ground-up bugs. Carmine, carminic acid, and cochineal extract are all red food coloring agents derived from the crushed carcasses of the female *Dactylopius coccus*, a Central and South American insect that gets its pigment by feasting on the red berries of the *Opuntia* cactus.

A Venezuelan television station was forced to remove *The Simpsons* from its morning programming because the government deemed the show "inappropriate" for children. They replaced it with reruns of *Baywatch*.

In an episode of *The Simpsons* entitled "E-I-E-I-D'oh," Homer creates "tomacco"—a highly addictive tomato-tobacco hybrid—when he fertilizes his fields with plutonium. Inspired by the episode and the *Scientific American* article from 1959 on which the concept is based, longtime *Simpsons* fan Rob Baur cultivated real tomacco in 2003.

Fly ash—a byproduct of coal-burning electric power plants—dumps one hundred times more radiation into the surrounding environment than a nuclear power plant producing the same amount of energy.

X-rays were discovered by Wilhelm Conrad Roentgen in 1895 while he was experimenting with electricity. He called them X-rays after the mathematical unknown *x* because he didn't understand what they were. (They are electromagnetic waves with very short wavelengths.) The first X-ray ever taken was of his wife's hand.

The phrase "smart alec" comes from Alec Hoag—celebrated pimp, thief, and confidence man operating in New York City in the 1840s. Hoag ran a con called the "panel game" in which prostitutes, their pimps, and a few cops on the take fleeced unsuspecting johns. Hoag earned the nickname "smart Alec" when the cops busted him for cutting them out of the action.

New York City still pays seven percent interest on long-maturing bonds issued over 140 years ago to fund an access road to a racetrack in the Bronx. Jerome Park—home of the first Belmont Stakes—and the road leading to it were the brainchild of Leonard W. Jerome, Winston Churchill's grandfather.

In 2007, a luxury pizza was introduced on the New York City restaurant scene for the astounding price of $1,000 a pie. Its toppings included caviar, lobster, and salmon roe.

Just one year later, the family restaurant Patsy's Pizza held a seventy-fifth anniversary party boasting a rollback to 1933 prices. So many bargain hunters lined up to grab ninety-cent twelve-ounce steaks that the NYPD was summoned to set up barricades. Patsy's employees eventually ended the party early and turned away the pizza lovers lined up around the block.

For a short period in 2003, many American restaurants featured "freedom fries" on their menus—a renaming of "French fries." Ostensibly, this was in reaction to France's vociferous opposition to America's invasion of Iraq. The phenomenon recalled the equally short-lived American trend during World War I of replacing "sauerkraut" with "liberty cabbage" as a way to express anti-German sentiment.

In 2008, Pepsi agreed to acknowledge on the labels of its Aquafina bottled water that the bottles contain public tap water. U.S. consumers bought 2.6 billion cases of bottled water in 2006.

If you eat sushi in the United States, you may have indirectly supported Rev. Sun Myung Moon's Unification Church. Rev. Moon laid out his plans to become "king of the ocean" in his 1980 speech "The Way of the Tuna." Through an umbrella company called True World Group, Moon's church owns boats and distribution centers, and supplies most of the nation's nearly nine thousand sushi restaurants.

FEBRUARY 29

A person born on February twenty-ninth is called a "leapling." A leapling's enjoyment of his "true" birthday every four years is used as a plot device in Gilbert and Sullivan's comic opera *The Pirates of Penzance*.

Before they called themselves the Hell's Angels, the legendary biker gang was known as The Pissed Off Bastards of Bloomington.

◆ ◆ ◆ ◆ ◆ ◆ ◆ ◆ ◆ ◆ ◆ ◆ ◆ ◆ ◆ ◆

The Goldwater Foundation, established by Congress in 1986, is a federally funded agency that provides academic scholarships to worthy students. Barry Goldwater was a conservative politician who opposed federal government spending on education.

In 2007, the Government Accountability Office discovered that the U.S. government had handed out $1.1 billion to dead farmers. In one case, continual payments were made to a farmer who had died in 1973.

In 2009, the Smithsonian's National Museum of American History opened a gold pocket watch that belonged to Abraham Lincoln and found graffiti on its inner workings. The watchmaker who repaired Lincoln's timepiece—the only Union sympathizer working in the shop—had inscribed: "Jonathan Dillon April 13–1861 Fort Sumpter was attacked by the rebels on the above date. J Dillon" and "April 13–1861 Washington thank God we have a government Jonth Dillon."

Though his current approval rating is at an all-time high, Abraham Lincoln couldn't always get the kind of PR a president wants—especially in his home state. In reaction to one of America's best-remembered political speeches, the Gettysburg Address, the Democratic-leaning *Chicago Times* had this to say: "The cheek of every American must tingle with shame as he reads the silly, flat and dishwatery utterances of the man who has to be pointed out to intelligent foreigners as the president of the United States." The Republican-oriented *New York Times* was more complimentary, pointing out that the audience interrupted the president five times with applause.

The first U.S. income tax was enacted to pay for the crippling costs of the Civil War and rescinded after the war when the Supreme Court declared the tax unconstitutional.

No taxation without representation" was the rallying cry that set off the American Revolution. Britain's total taxation of the colonies in 1776 is estimated to have been just two percent of personal income, whereas the average tax bite on American workers today is thirty percent.

◆ ◆ ◆ ◆ ◆ ◆ ◆ ◆ ◆ ◆ ◆ ◆ ◆ ◆ ◆ ◆

In 1913, Congress amended the Sixteenth Amendment and paved the way for the reinstitution of a federal income tax. Nevertheless, each year between fifty and one hundred thousand Americans challenge its legality. In 2001, the IRS created the Frivolous Return Program to deal with tax scofflaws. Unofficially, the IRS calls this "the funny box."

Tax preparation company H&R Block filed its taxes incorrectly. It was forced to restate earnings for fiscal years 2004, 2005, and part of 2006 due to underreporting of its state income tax liability.

The largest denomination banknote ever issued into circulation was the Hungarian 100 quintillion (100,000,000,000,000,000,000) *pengo*, minted in July 1946 during an extreme case of hyperinflation. There were too many zeros to depict them on the banknote.

In 2009, annual inflation in Zimbabwe ran at the astounding rate of 89.7 sextillion percent. At 4 percent inflation, it takes roughly eighteen years for money to lose half of its value. With inflation at 89.7 sextillion percent, it takes just twenty-four hours.

David Rice Atchison legally became the president for a twenty-four-hour period, even though he was never elected to office or sworn in. President James Knox Polk was scheduled to step down from office at noon on Sunday, March 4, 1849, but president-elect Zachary Taylor refused to be sworn in on a Sunday. Atchison, president pro tem of the Senate, was the constitutional stopgap.

America's first fireworks-studded celebration of the Fourth of July occurred in 1777—one year after the signing of the Declaration of Independence and a full six years before the end of the Revolutionary War.

After killing Alexander Hamilton in a duel and trying to steal Louisiana Purchase land in an attempt to crown himself Emperor of Mexico (he was acquitted of treason), Aaron Burr fled to Europe in self-imposed exile (and to escape his creditors), where he tried to convince Napoléon to conquer Florida.

Cinco de Mayo commemorates not Mexico's independence but the Battle of Puebla, in which General Zaragosa bested Napoléon III's forces—that while fighting with half as many men. This 1862 battle was the first loss for the French army since Waterloo, when Napoléon Bonaparte, Napoléon III's uncle, was defeated.

General George Armstrong Custer was the "goat" of the United States Military Academy at West Point in 1861. A "goat" is the cadet who finishes last in his class.

Until 1912, mail was delivered seven days a week. As the postal service grew in popularity and usage in the 1800s, local religious leaders noticed a decline in Sunday morning church attendance due to local post offices doubling as gathering places. These leaders appealed to the government to intervene and close post offices on Sundays.

With the onset of World War I, President Woodrow Wilson brought sheep to graze on the White House lawns in order to save the expense of mowing the expansive grounds. The wool was donated to the Red Cross.

The phrase "basket case" was introduced into common parlance during World War I. It referred to a quadruple amputee.

During World War II, some American and British battleships were covered in elaborate, brightly colored cubist designs in an effort to flummox enemy torpedoes. The dramatic paint jobs were called "Dazzle Paint" and "Razzle Dazzle."

U.S. Air Force research laboratory documents testify to a theoretical non-lethal chemical weapon informally known as the "gay bomb," or "poof bomb." In the New Discoveries Needed section, the documents acknowledge that chemicals causing homosexual behavior are "not currently known." The reports also propose a chemical weapon that would give the enemy bad breath, a "heavy sweating bomb," and a "flatulence bomb." These would allow Americans to sniff out combatants. Stench was considered fairly damaging to enemy morale as well.

C*asu marzu* is a Sardinian delicacy colloquially known as "maggot cheese." *Casu marzu* is Pecorino fermented to near-decomposition by the introduction of cheese fly larvae (*Piophila casei*), lending a soft texture with seeping liquid called *lagrima* (Sardinian for "tears"). The maggots can launch themselves up to six inches, often leaping for the eyes of anyone enjoying the cheese. Sardinians too squeamish to consume live maggots seal an opened cheese round in a paper sack. When the "popcorn" sound of suffocating maggots leaping against the bag ceases, the cheese is ready to eat.

Ingesting *Casu marzu* carries the risk of intestinal larval infection, symptoms of which include nausea, vomiting, abdominal pain, and bloody diarrhea. Additionally, the larvae have powerful mouthhooks that can lacerate stomach linings or intestinal walls as the maggots attempt to bore through internal organs. The government of Sardinia has outlawed the cheese, but it's possible to obtain *Casu marzu* on the black market for twice the price of Pecorino.

Swedes eat rotten herring. Norwegians eat *lutefisk*—cod soaked in lye. Icelanders eat sharks that have being buried in gravel for up to six months. Most Scandinavians chase these healthfully questionable delicacies with strong liquor.

Sharks have two penises, or "claspers."

Relative to body size, the barnacle has the largest penis in the animal kingdom. Not only can the crustacean's penis grow to eight times the length of its body, it can also change shape in response to changing environmental conditions.

Female ducks have faux vaginas they can distend for unwanted suitors.

The duck-billed platypus has been referred to as proof that God has a sense of humor. Genetically speaking, the platypus is an evolutionary missing link. While technically classified as a mammal because it lactates and has fur, its genome contains DNA found only in birds and reptiles.

When the first stuffed platypus made its way to Europe in 1798, British scientists believed they were the victim of a hoax by an Asian taxidermist. Convinced that a duck's beak had been sewn onto a beaver, they checked the platypus' cheeks for stitches.

Seahorses and pipefish (freshwater seahorses) are the only known species in which males become pregnant. Seahorses are generally monogamous, and during a male's two- to three-week pregnancy a mating pair will engage in daily greetings that involve courting dances, mutual color changes, and promenades.

A water flea called the spiny helmet daphnia poses a challenge to Darwin's theory of natural selection. Fleas with identical DNA sequences can be born with or without the protective spiny helmet. If one parent was exposed to predators, offspring are born with helmets; otherwise they are born without helmets, but can grow them in response to a threat. According to Darwin's theory, it should take generations of natural selection to produce such a genetic change.

◆ ◆ ◆ ◆ ◆ ◆ ◆ ◆ ◆ ◆ ◆ ◆ ◆ ◆ ◆

Fleas that live on dogs jump higher than fleas that live on cats.

A flea can jump six hundred times an hour for three days straight, each jump the equivalent of a human being leaping over the Empire State Building.

During jumps, fleas reach peak acceleration of 140 Gs —more than thirty times the gravitational force endured by astronauts during the launch of the *Saturn V* moon rocket.

In addition to having eight arms, octopi have three hearts—two that pump blood through the gills and a third to pump blood through the body.

Everyone knows that spiders have eight legs, but they also have eight eyes. These are mostly for show, however, as spiders have terrible vision and must rely almost exclusively on their sense of touch.

Researchers in Antarctica were able to grow an eight-million-year-old bacterium extracted from the oldest ice on Earth. As the polar ice caps melt, ancient bacteria and viruses dormant for millions of years will slowly come back to life.

Dirt is good for you. As any toddler instinctively knows, eating dirt (which contains myriad bacteria) helps boost fledgling immune systems.

Plants have family values. Researchers in Canada discovered that plants from the same species of beach-dwelling wildflower grew aggressively alongside unrelated neighbors but were more cooperative when they shared soil with their siblings. According to the researchers, this suggests that plants, though lacking cognition and memory, are capable of complex social interactions.

In 2002, scientists discovered a new genus and species of centipede (*Nannarrup hoffmani*) in New York City's Central Park—the first new species discovered there in over a century.

Researchers in London found that urban robins have taken to singing at night because it is too noisy for their melodies to be heard during the daytime.

Recent research shows that marijuana may actually keep your memory sharp. Tetrahydrocannabinol (THC), the psychoactive ingredient in marijuana, reduces inflammation and stimulates the production of new brain cells, thereby enhancing recall and helping to ward off Alzheimer's disease.

Smoking is worse for your health than poverty. In a recent study in Scotland, scientists found that rich smokers were more likely to die young than non-smokers without means.

The strange symptoms that ignited the Salem Witch Trials—hallucinations, incomprehensible speech, and odd skin sensations—were most likely caused by ergot poisoning from infected rye bread. Ergot (*Claviceps purpurea*), a fungus that infects cereal grasses like wheat and rye, contains potent chemicals known as ergot alkaloids, including lysergic acid, from which LSD is derived, and ergotamine, now used to treat migraine headaches.

John Pemberton, the founder of Coca-Cola, put cocaine in his soft drink in reaction to the temperance movement. The original formula was for French Coca Wine but under pressure from the growing backlash against alcohol use, Pemberton dropped the alcohol but kept the coca and the kola.

The original recipe for the soft drink 7-Up contained lithium citrate, a mood stabilizing drug used to treat manic depression, now called bipolar disorder. 7-Up was launched two weeks before the stock market crash of 1929.

You can fatally overdose on water. Current guidelines limit fluid intake during times of heavy sweating to 1.5 quarts per hour.

In the first century AD, Nero levied a urine tax (*vectigal urinae*) on the lower classes. Urine served as an important ingredient in a number of chemical processes. It was used to soften hides for tanning or to dissolve excess fatty tissue and flesh that remained on the hide after skinning. It was also used as a source of ammonia by Roman launderers to clean and whiten woolen togas.

According to the National Woolen Museum in Western Wales, human urine was used to prepare raw wool for the spinners. Locals, often on their way home from the pub, were paid a penny a gallon for their urine. Methodists were paid two pennies a gallon because they didn't drink alcohol so their urine was purer and thus more valuable.

A sixty-five-year-old railwayman who fell into a coma following an accident in communist Poland woke up nineteen years later, in 2007, to democracy and a market economy.

The next year, a seventy-eight-year-old blind man bowled a perfect 300.

In 2008, a construction crane in New York City collapsed and destroyed a four-story townhouse. Among the rubble were the remains of Fubar, a tavern that had operated in the bottom floor of the building. Often used by radiomen in World War II, FUBAR is an acronym for "F$@%ed Up Beyond All Recognition."

George Bush (1796–1859), a liberal academic and journalist and forebear of two conservative presidents, wrote the first English-language book on Islam.

Casanova, the Brothers Grimm, Ben Franklin, Mao Tse-Tung, and J. Edgar Hoover were all librarians.

Mussolini developed revolutionary fascism in Italy with Margherita Sarfatti, his Jewish mistress. He kicked Sarfatti out of his bed and Italy when he passed race laws in 1938, hoping to curry favor with Hitler's Germany on the eve of World War II.

While on the run during the great exodus, the Jews ate foie gras. They had learned how to force-feed ducks and geese from their Egyptian oppressors, who had been fattening fowl since 2500 BC.

Some ants are slavers. *Protomagnathus americanus*, for example, raid the colonies of other ant species, kill all the adults, and steal as much larvae as they can carry back to their own nest. Once the stolen ants mature, they assume their masters' odor and are forced to work for the

slaver queen, even taking part in raids. Ants from the genus *Temnothorax*, however, rebel. Rather than tend to the brood as all drones must, the mature slaves neglect and deliberately kill their captors' pupae. In cases of uprisings, two-thirds of the slavers' colony die before hatching.

In 2008, Joseph Stalin was voted third most popular Russian. Stalin is credited with the murders of up to sixty million people—more than four times the number of deaths attributed to Adolf Hitler.

With 620,000 dead, the Civil War was the bloodiest war in American history. During roughly the same period (1850–1864) in China, a Christian convert named Hong Xiuquan led a revolt to eradicate Confucianism, Buddhism, and folk religions and replace them with a Christian utopia he called the Taiping Heavenly Kingdom. The Taiping Rebellion was eventually put down after an estimated twenty to forty million Chinese men, women, and children were killed.

A language dies every two weeks. Of the seven thousand languages spoken in the world today, linguists claim half are in danger of extinction and likely to disappear during this century.

The most ubiquitous typeface in history, Times New Roman, came about as a result of a damning letter to the editor back in 1931. After criticizing the British *Times* for being badly printed and typographically out of date, Stanley Morison was commissioned by the newspaper to create the serif typeface.

The three preeminent American brewers—Joseph Schlitz, Frederick Pabst, and Aldolphus Busch (Budweiser)—all married into the business. All three of their fathers-in-law owned unprofitable breweries that Schlitz, Pabst, and Busch took over and turned into an entire industry.

Oktoberfest was originally held to finish up the dregs of *Märzen*, or "March beer." To last through the summer, extra alcohol was added to the brew, and the beer was stored in caves. *Lager* is the German word for "storage."

S ake is a beer.

C offee prevents dementia.

R ed wine extends life.

In 2009, Mexican drug lord Joaquin "El Chapo" Guzman Loeraug, worth an estimated $1 billion, thanked United States politicians for keeping drugs illegal. He is reported to have said, "I couldn't have gotten so stinking rich without George Bush, George Bush Jr., Ronald Reagan, even El Presidente Obama, none of them have the cojones to stand up to all the big money that wants to keep this stuff illegal. From the bottom of my heart, I want to say, Gracias amigos, I owe my whole empire to you."

Based on the data from a 2008 Gallup World Poll, the ten happiest countries are:

10. Belgium

9. Norway

8. New Zealand

7. Switzerland

6. Canada

5. Ireland

4. Sweden

3. The Netherlands

2. Finland

1. Denmark

In 2008, a Texas mom gave birth to "twins" from two different dads. The boys, who are technically fraternal half-brothers, were the result of "heteropaternal superfecundation," which basically means "different fathers, multiple fertilizations." In order for this to happen, a woman has to release two eggs in the same month then have sex with two different partners within 48 hours. Although heteropaternal superfecundation is common among cats and dogs, it is exceedingly rare in humans. There are fewer than a dozen cases on record.